A History of the River

A History of the River

poems by James Applewhite

James Applewhite (signature)

LOUISIANA STATE UNIVERSITY PRESS
Baton Rouge and London   1993

First printing
02 01 00 99 98 97 96 95 94 93   5 4 3 2 1

Designer: Amanda McDonald Key
Typeface: Palatino
Typesetter: G&S Typesetters, Inc.
Printer and binder: Thomson–Shore, Inc.

Library of Congress Cataloging-in-Publication Data
Applewhite, James.
     A history of the river : poems / by James Applewhite.
        p.   cm.
     ISBN 0-8071-1815-X (alk. paper.—ISBN 0-8071-1816-8 (pbk. :
     alk. paper)
        1. Neuse River Valley (N.C.)—History—Poetry.   I. Title.
     PS3551.P67H57   1993
     811'.54—dc20   92-28213
                                                           CIP

Grateful acknowledgment is made to the editors of the following publications, in which many of these poems first appeared: *Chronicle of Higher Education* ("A Wilson County Farmer"), *New England Review* ("Imaginary Photograph"; "Slender Pines in Smoky Light"), *Now This* ("Horsepower"; "Without Destination"), *Ohio Review* ("Accident of Inheritance"), *Poet and Critic* ("A Father and Son"; "What You Don't See Is There"), *Poetry* ("Storm in the Briar Patch"), *Sewanee Review* ("Among Names of My Fathers"; "The Autumn Potato"), *Shenandoah* ("A Change of Sky"), *Southern Review* ("After *Winslow Homer's Images of Blacks*"; "Almon and Jane"; "Echoes of Origin"; "Home Team"; "Remembering William Blackburn in a Leaf"), *Turnstile* ("Making Tobacco Money"), and *Verse* ("Time at Seven Springs").

Publication of this book has been supported by a grant from the National Endowment for the Arts in Washington, D.C., a federal agency.

for Jan

That these were the years before a revolution, a cataclysm, not only in how people made a living but in how they thought about the natural world, and, inevitably, themselves in relation to it, no one had an inkling. Tenants still went down to their wood-burning tobacco barn at night and added wood to the furnace, checking that the fire neither went out nor got so high that the barn burned.

—Linda Flowers, *Throwed Away: Failures of Progress in Eastern North Carolina*

CONTENTS

A History of the River

Among Names of My Fathers

The iron fence protecting your stones has spent
    its form in rust, the briars sharper curved
than its twisted wires. What these inscriptions meant
    has eroded also, though I read that one of you served
the Confederate States. I know that your bones rest here,
    I read your initials, wives, scriptures, the year

of your births and deaths. But the distance between us
    seems unbridgeable, you lie in deeds I can't approve.
Your owning of lands and men is history, fabulous
    though true. The field you mark was sold, your graves
now protected by habit and respect, that rust in this air
    acid with change, with T.V., highways, developments, new wars.

Only this season seems to sympathize, sky annealed
    by fall above the bronze-banded century-canopies
of hickories. They stand together beyond this soybean field,
    old warriors whispering in foliage, temporal sentries
by a boundary stream. Beyond is the land I'll own,
    the rust-rich furrows where tobacco and corn are sown.

I kneel as if for prayer or digging, to unearth
    an ancestry the shafts and CSA marker parody:
monoliths erupting out of a past as alien to the self
    as a tree from clay, inscribed with dark identity.
I study a label the years conspired to write,
    a made word in this roseate, fictionalizing light.

I stand my ground of fathers, of a buried fame,
    my wrenched heart pulled two ways, toward
life as a stranger to graves, toward fields' time
    dense with shed names. A charred headboard
waits like an unwritten slate, to be filled by one
    intent to read himself a man, one of a line.

MAKING TOBACCO MONEY

In those days, the silver in a dollar meant
        material for a spoon or a ring. Hand labor
showed itself in wrought iron, scrollwork on porches,
        spokes shaved and fitted into wheels, which iron
rims tightened as they cooled. Whatever excess value
        might arise was simple to behold: corncribs
husbanding energy in kerneled ears the color of
        sunlight, and animals more numerous in the spring,
stock surviving the winter's rain in barns roofed with
        galvanized iron. People accepted the land's
ownership as a fact of life. Uncleared borders
        toward swamps offered more space for more labor.
Pines replenished themselves over exhausted pastures.
        Broom sedge colonized, its sunset-tan extending
in feathery ranks homogeneous as wheat. Evergreen seedlings
        then bulked up gradually: green, irregular pyramids
increasing in value year by year, no pulpwood needed
        for paper, no economic motive to notice their teenaged
gangling into thickets where the farmer's son might
        construct his house for practice; his cabin of saplings.
These folk identified themselves not by wealth on paper but
        by visible achievements of their hands: the farmhouse
white in its trees, the fields around engraved with rows,
        the corn uniformly flourishing. Neatness in washing
and ironing—bedsheets boiled and then pressed with flat-
        irons heated on the stove, scrupulous cleanliness
in canning—were their signatures of decency and order.
        Observing the strict, essential wisdom of hog killing,
they rendered the lard in pots set on flaming billets;
        mixed meat and spices in a hand-cranked grinder,
extruded the sausage into guts scraped thin as a condom;
        preserved the hams and shoulders by rubbing in salt,
peppered and smoked the hides that contracted to leather.
        So the farmer accumulated value, as he and his wife
and children were able: preserving the rich peaches,
        their yellow-round sides like egg yolks, showing more
deliciously through glass in the pantry than gold to
        a miser in his vault. When all knew the labor
of putting-in time, when croppers bent low for tobacco,
        then up the stalk, easier for the best middle leaf;
the looping and hanging and tending the curing fires—
        log barns fueled with hardwood cut and split

from lowlands in winter—the hand grading of leaves
   after the ordering, when moisture was absorbed in pits;
the final binding of the fragrant bundle into "hands"
   long as forearms, to be piled on the warehouse floor;
when all knew this toil, and the temptation not to
   perform it one more year, then shiftless backslidings
into need seemed blamable as evil. So the barns
   loomed up at twilight, squarer and higher for their
foundation spaces than the two-story houses;
   assertions of order against chaos, the furnacelike
masonry showing its fiery half-oval, under heavy,
   green-reeking leaf—looped shapes hanging from the
tobacco sticks, primordial, slime-colored, odious
   as catfish, to be converted into civilized tender,
become material for a gesture, the pinching from
   a snuffbox or rolling of cigarette. So a frontier
vagueness was transmuted under intense scrutiny
   from base green leaf to a fragrance golden as money.

MEN CROSSING A STREET

Southern history, unlike American, includes large components of frustration,
failure, and defeat.

—C. Vann Woodward

Two southern men, in their tinlike
    khaki pants, hurry their stiff shanks
getting out of the path of a car—in this
    their own town and street, this their
homeplace to walk at ease, if ever in life
    at leisure. I read in their faces of
sun-enforced wrinkles these clay soils
    eroded by seasons, where self-effacing
gestures of men like part of the setting
    depress kinfolk of losers of battles
closer to the fields' levels. They stand aside,
    self-sufficient, proud, not respecting
their stature as special and to be waited for,
    not giving the stranger a moment to be
generous in delay, not accepting the charity
    of his pause or the praise of his eyes
on their face-furrows noble in ruin—
    as if admiration were not to be taken
from those not privy to the condition
    of hard work and no name, of fame
in hearing of family only, of sons, whose
    known fortune will be land unrolled
around carved stone by these wills.

Gradually, poles had edged their way, shouldering
            stretched arcs of wire beside farm roads: red clay
for the big-wheeled roadsters to slither in, when rainy weeks
            made rivers of silt. So that families near low places
expected to be awakened in the middle of the night by
            the frightened young couple, asking for a tow from
the mule team. But the lines of current went out, gradually,
            and oil lamps winked out like dying stars, though the old
ones used this power reverently: one sixty-watt bulb
            in a room, turned out punctually when the last person
went up for the night—the unfrosted glass holding filament-
            pattern that printed the retina, when the half-light
came again, and the hallway lamp cast marks of shadow—
            straightish joints in tongue-and-groove paneling, grave
lines of the houses, somber constructions to box out drafts,
            hold heat, display glass shelves in the company parlor,
where figurines in porcelain skirts could deny the pressure
            of labor, clothes washed on corrugated boards, in galvanized
washtubs. But power brought enameled washers, with wringers,
            so that clothes half-squeezed of water could be pinned on lines,
to freeze and maybe blow down, or hang for days, board-solid,
            overalls like a paper-doll cutout of the farmer, a silhouette
with sand-colored abrasions of his labor. And macadam
            began to pave over crossing roads in towns, to extend
navigable surfaces into a landscape fertile with mud
            in spring, thick with dust in heat-sterile August, to plume
behind the farm truck, inscribing its solitary, unaltering
            way in a cloud magnified by distance, like an expanding
destiny. The train would come through in the time before sleep,
            when families lay under cotton quilts which weighted
their bodies without warming—vulnerable there to a loneliness
            its whistle embodied: a tone of having come out of nowhere.
But gradually the motorcars assembled, with whitewall tires
            and hubcaps, glass-enclosed cabins with horsehair upholstery
as on a sofa in a parlor. People arrived in new models sporty
            with rumble seats and running boards, had themselves
photographed at church school picnics and family reunions,
            on Sundays lazy with heat-glaze, beside the pond fed by springs,
where an overflow flowered its artesian sparkle. There the tin-
            roofed shelter on posts, the pier into water for diving,

the women in their modest, one-piece suits, but showing whole
    thighs now, armored against shame by the helmetlike
bathing caps. The men wore their decent outfits, trunks and
    shoulder-showing tank tops, grinning into sunlight, the time-
flight stopped by dazzle from the shirt of one who would not
    go in the water or shed his white sleeves in the heat. His
features were unfazed by progress. He looked beyond the temporary
    gathering to see the mules still waiting in their pastures
for breaking land and harrowing, for cultivating corn hills.
    A few red Farmall tractors dotted the edges of his vision
as comprehensively he took in woods line and field rise, oaks
    over homesteads in leaf-clouds like thunderheads. He saw the
tractors as toys, the sky always as source of change, and of seasons—
    cloud shadows bruising the corn, before bristles of downpour
released it into sparkling. Sky was the source of November rain
    when rivers and farm ponds filled up again, and of snow
by fence posts and troughs, china white, of the March winds
    which dried fields as the farmer was plowing, sent dust across
counties, yellowing the highway—paved, despite his skepticism.

In obedience and ignorance, okra
    stalks, gaunt as prisoners, stand
where screens only keep the flies in.
    Dry season and the boy's father
slaps him for no reason it seems—
    rutted landscape fallen to ruin,
pokeweed veined like a hand
    where the scraps of laundry hang,
flap like the wrung-necked rag of
    a chicken in its arcs. Storm
seems a long time coming and strong
    when it dooms down. Spark
crack connects the sky and land
    with copper-green scar in the eye,
as the cat trembles, the three fish
    wait to be cleaned. The lean-tos
lean into the wind, lean as bean-
    poles, the beans dangling, jangled
like wind chimes, while farmers damn
    the hail as it holes tobacco: broad
as banana leaves, like small roofs but
    pierced now, a punctured infantry.
After, he goes the rounds of his fields, each
    hill shredded, a mimic-man, a sham of
what life might be—ghost of a crop to go
    up from a match in cloud and
gesture, not shiver here, broken, long
    hours of raising ruined in his eyes.

From the arched Philco with its speaker like a Gothic window
        came news from the sky. Later, newsreels showed the *Arizona*
hulled over, burning. The P-40's and slender-tailed B-17's in
        their peacetime markings lay crumpled in piles. The sky
became accelerator of change—no longer the river with
        its slow hieroglyphic, its evolution from sailing craft
and log raft to steam-huffed packet. Not the railroad
        with its comprehensible, coal-fired engine in its black
piston-shape, not even the new year's models of Chryslers
        and Buicks, but an airborne sound from the distance: Pearl
Harbor, jewel-lustrous, catastrophic syllables. Volunteers
        watched from Forest Service tower and rooftop, with manuals
to aid them, though the middle-aged eyes behind glasses confused one
        aircraft with another. But the boy on the roof of his father's
station recognized each type as by instinct—in the one-room
        house all windows, as he waited for apocalyptic sightings.
He imagined a desperate combat the whole country entered in,
        his somnolent South now wired by the phone line that
began at his own left hand to the military fathers, whose
        planes changed as quickly as the broadcasts: P-38's and
B-17's, the milk-jug P-47's, moving through the new marks,
        with armor and self-sealing tanks, machine guns and
cannon, stabilizer-fins extended. Young men training
        at Seymour Johnson nearby strained to learn control
of a fighter like a winged locomotive. One of these P-47's
        crashed in the edge of his county. He went with his father.
The boulderlike motor had broken from its mounts, an engine
        of two thousand horsepower rolling like the Juggernaut of
wartime, bowling down pine trees, letting in sunlight
        through the central, violated grove, toward the hollow,
frangible body. This Thunderbolt of a technical rhetoric
        in a pastoral accumulated too vividly for scrutiny
illuminated a fuselage broken at the cockpit: a pilot's
        seat stark as an electric chair, where the throne
of this new succession stood jellied with blood.

WATER FROM THE LAMP BOTTLE

A few months later SEVEN SPRINGS HOTEL was opened. Soon it was the mecca for society in Eastern Carolina. Fine carriages, plumed hats, tight breeches and bat-wing ties lent the resort a grace which is lacking today.
—*Some Facts About Seven Springs Waters*, 1940

> The grandfather's ten-gallon demijohn
>   is stoppered with a lamp, a shade
> disguising the mouth that blabbed out
>   Seven Springs water. The sources of those
> seven trickles—each supposedly with
>   its own curative properties—were boxed
> already by concrete, enclosed within octagonal
>   latticework: wet tunnels in a wall, origin
> of the sheen that overspread the floor slab
>   like polish on marble. The Neuse drifted
> darkly, smooth, enigmatic, seen by a child
>   refreshed after drinking from the dipper,
> feet tingling from the cold, surprised by a frog
>   in the springhouse. Those beginnings that
> brightened concrete, to be taken home in your own
>   formulation in the oversized bottle, seemed
> to him the source of the river. It slid there,
>   slick against the underside of so much air—
> air possessing, in the distance of its width,
>   a blue tint of accumulated haze; air wet
> with vapor, temperature eighties or nineties, clouds
>   casting down white impressions of their bulks,
> flattened there, stylized in two dimensions.
>   So the scene itself seemed dual: a tintype
> photograph versus the vivid present a child
>   feels, scampering from a frog, desiring
> Spanish moss as it waved in grandfatherly
>   beards, spears on that swarthy surface: a corded,
> sweat-oiled portrait of a life past representing.
>   Fists and forearms of black men had worked
> in strokes like pistons so that the steam barge
>   could huff its vapor. The somnolent reflections
> of bends fixed willows and the darting dragonfly.

HOME TEAM

There was a stillness about the games, afternoons,
        something to be decided, but in suspension—a runner
taking his lead as the pitcher eyed him suspiciously,
        the outfielders glancing back at the bushes thirty
feet to their rear, edging in a little, trying to remember
        the soft spots, where a line drive wouldn't bounce up.
Thunderheads building in the sky enveloped the scene within
        an elemental light. The thickening, varnishlike quality
of water in air, and heat—the pure clarity beginning to
        congeal—would capture this space at the edge of a village,
gathering its figures into one impression, while a fly ball
        hit long toward right center hung up against the base
of a cloud, the crowd rising to its feet as the runner on first
        broke joyously for second, toward home. Charles Boykin,
coming around the bases, grinned with the mouths of small boys
        under the tree, their biceps thicker as they looked at his.
So the game and those summers continued. But Charlie Justice
        played for the Redskins, his figure ghostly in the electronic
snow of T.V.—not on a field near the one that Willie
        Mozingo had plowed, before he took his chunky body into
far left field, a two-legged gleam in his cream-colored uniform,
        as afternoon deepened and the slanting sun made balls hard
to judge but he caught them anyway, back in the broom sedge.
        Fred Pittman signed the minor-league contract and people
went to Wilson to see him. The diamond was left to high-
        school games, to frog creak and owl whoop in midsummer
evenings, and the lightning bugs coming on in a space that
        held the stars. Houses in sight of the diamond oak
lit up their windows with the glow of T.V. Always a few
        farm boys, not risking injury, hit rocks toward the trees
with broomsticks, or prevailed on a younger brother to throw
        them one more pitch down the middle, so they could drive
the baseball over the weeded ditch, out of the pasture.

THE YEARS AGO

She remembers him building a basket of splinters.
    Doves walked close to their doorstep, pecking.
A string he fingered triggered his birdtrap.
    She watched them roast in their feathers, a fire
on the hearth of splinters, him coughing, satisfied in
    his beard and bitterness—this man her father
too short-winded for work in the fields, making a cage
    with his words and caresses, the tiny drumstick
of the dove, roasted. Her mother pretended not to know,
    worn out with labor, silent so long as her
daughter was hairless and doll-like. The bulged thing
    hurt her but children learn secrecy, her wide eyes
appalled by the cage-fall but intrigued by the terror,
    the bird's frantic wing-flaps, then stillness.

HORSEPOWER

A vast precision extended its language to small-town
      garages, stations where gasoline and fan belts were sold.
The moral rectitude of fathers became measurements by
      micrometers to the ten-thousandth of an inch.
A motive force hidden as not even in steam locomotives
      hurled the postwar models to a hundred miles an hour,
manifolds sucking an aromatic to the fiery eight cylinders.
      Pistons working in their film of oil now whirled in secret,
connected to a black elastic that erased old hours of distance.
      He remembered how son of banker or farmer, agent or clerk,
had tested himself and his father's machine to the limit
      along the two-mile stretch from Saratoga, to reach
maximum velocity crossing the bridge over Toisnot Swamp,
      water beside the timbers suddenly blasted by a rush-roar
that made bullfrogs jump and submerged the turtles, while
      an unknown dark tonnage with a family's chief hope at
the chancy wheel prepared to take the curve into town,
      tires whining asphalt at the limit of their adhesion.
He remembered the posters for stock car races, them moving from
      the dirt tracks of county fairgrounds to paved ovals
and crowds, the ex-bootleggers and shadetree mechanics
      giving way to the skilled, professional drivers whose
homey drawls were preserved like Confederate flags on
      license plates. But his own uncle, a Methodist minister,
crippled by arthritis, had driven his Chevrolet with an upright
      dignity, unable to turn his head as he was backing.
He misses this uncle of hymns and texts, in his pinstriped suit,
      not moving like the others with their cars in curves,
disdaining, in his memory, this giving in to the machine.

A Wilson County Farmer

The mercury-vapor yard light on a pole
    comes on automatically at dusk, triggered
it seems by the television's phosphorescent glow in
    the front room, seen incongruously through those
sashes and panes from just after the Civil War.
    The middle-aged farmer standing in shadow of this
unnatural light before his packhouse, still smoking
    a Lucky, just a few in any day now, sees
heads of his wife and daughter-in-law through the
    window, and the grandson's occasional, ball-quick
passage through color, and thinks maybe he has survived
    too long. Life is easier, maybe, with MH-30
to inhibit suckers, the tractor-drawn harvesters,
    where croppers ride close to the ground, breaking
off leaves, clipping them into the reeled chains. But hands
    are undependable, and without his blood kin,
a man couldn't hardly be sure of a harvest crew.
    Some use the migrants, hard-working, ignorant
of the ways of tobacco. With the quotas, the declining
    prices, every day more news about cancer, this man
who learned tobacco from his father, who himself couldn't
    read and write, looks far across at red Antares
over the swamp woods there beyond the highway, not knowing
    what star he is seeing, and feels his station in this
place lit by blue light and T.V. as odd and as lonely.

The Autumn Potato

The sweet potato, later than tomatoes,
    looked of a paler blood, though each
vegetable flesh seemed human—these
    root-shapes bulged for the fingers,

like bellies and butts of newborns.
    The basketsful kept by a family
lit a sweet coal-smoldering in the pantry,
    as sugar cured each inside darker,

a bond between brother and sister.
    They imagined them cooked with molasses,
brown-thick as the creek's low water;
    tacky, their candy, a home-flesh

kept from all others. The marshmallowed
    dish would mean Christmas, the cloth
rimmed with lace that she wanted, a rifle
    for him if he was lucky. The buttock-

curved potatoes lay binned, still
    burning their ripening in the pantry,
as he imagined her body in the panties
    and looked beyond fields of the family:

anticipating the bus ride to Norfolk,
    or Raleigh, leaving what would never
be returned to, carrying his bag of biscuits,
    the cold cooked family potato. He'd marry

his appetite to others, ladies with underwear
    from stores, and hose, a sheerness never
imagined, where flour sacks had furnished
    her dresses. His taste home cooking

had flavored would favor the sweeter
    potato, until a wife would serve him yams
at Christmas: ripe flesh color in a dish,
    under marshmallows like tattered lace.

ALMON AND JANE

The brother and his sister, unreconciled to the present,
    sat on the porch of her husband's house and talked
while the war went on: two southerners troubled by their past.
    Though they had traveled from parsonage to parsonage,
responsible too soon for their brothers and sister, though
    childhood with Father and his horse, the buggy he
fell under, had been painful and anxious, their emotions
    yearned back to those days. Jane sighed for a crystal
graciousness, for vases and punch bowls, sterling flatware,
    for the dignity of Father as District Superintendent. Almon
described the out-of-the-way places where he'd taught high school:
    Harker's Island, Buxton, Hatteras Village; and the fishermen's
children, ones who'd never seen an orange. His sister insisted
    on a hurricane when she was herself a teacher, at Aurora—
how upstairs the pine needles had lashed against her window,
    the house a paper lantern, trembling around three women.
The boy her son drank it in eagerly, this lingering history
    lived beside rivers; and from another uncle also, the lawyer
at Washington, that waterfront littered with wooden-hulled vessels,
    before the hectic outboard motors had changed the sound
and the pace on the wide Pamlico, when cylinders amidships,
    coupled to a shaft, had stuttered a slower beat across
the water. Almon was obsessed by one-lane bridges and
    their wooden reverberation when a buggy had passed over;
by Confederate stones in cemeteries. When summer storms
    frightened away his sister, he and her son stayed bravely in
their chairs, as air grew gray and lightning seamed a purple
    beyond the trees. When rain sheeted down from the over-
hanging eaves, Rommel and North Africa faded into Lee and
    Grant and the wild yell of soldiers, as men in a living
wave assaulted Cemetery Ridge, into the muskets, his words
    hardly making an issue of bravery, full mostly of the long,
agonized cry of so much enduring. The wounds, amputated limbs,
    the jolting back from Gettysburg in wagons, let the defeated
southern voices hang out there over their region in a ghost
    of loss, like a train whistle in the middle of the night:
the South unable to walk forward in its own right on those
    stumps and crutches. The boy felt only the cry in its lungs,
dark and wild as the wind's mane when the hurricane brushed
    against a window and a river history lived in the storm's rush.

TRIBUTARY BRANCHES

The wires hung taut along country roads,
      their poles canted, the creosote color of rivers.
Would a time ever come to assemble a consciousness
      of a life which had never known itself? The fragments
that haunted him—faces in albums, maps showing
      routes of steamboats—collided with chromium images,
airliners fragmented among toothpaste and pantyhose,
      in a mirroring quicksilver shot electronically
through the domed, dumb mind from horizon to horizon
      over fields: a simultaneous, unbelieved moment,
so that the reality eluded perception. Stories were
      forgotten, this new time carried in the air,
disguising the trees of genetic coding, of relatives
      scattered among tributary branches of the Neuse,
cousins and uncles along Contentnea, Toisnot, relatives
      by marriage in Grifton, Ayden, Shelmerdine.

ACCIDENT OF INHERITANCE

The galvanized shelters hold tractors, and the fields
    are in good order: the stalks cut and plowed under
last fall, after the cropping. The bulk barns stand
    together like a miniature trailer park, a permanent
shelter over them. Formerly only the brush on rafters kept
    the handers and loopers from passing out, those days
of ninety-five degrees. Now progress has done what it can,
    short of air-conditioning the fields. This recalcitrant
climate had seemed fit medium for his father's stature: six-
    foot, sinewy, with staring blue eyes, like Confederate
infantrymen, photographed. His expression penetrated excuses or
    problems, his Adam's apple moving as he swallowed and
gave orders. He never chewed tobacco, but his jaw ridged out
    as if a quid were there and his words had an acrid edge.
The grown son, tall as his father, thicker, feels himself
    caught between two worlds. He drives away to meetings on
soil conservation but lives beside the homeplace in his expanded
    mobile home—his office inside there, with personal computer
carrying records of corn and soybean production, in his
    bedroom a few relics of the failed first marriage, panties
in the bottom of a drawer and he can't remember whether
    they belonged to his wife or were left by a girl friend.
His mother was driving, his father recovering from surgery,
    doing well with the bypass. The car lights blinded her,
she pulled out anyway. His neck was broken. Now the son
    dreads the coming season. The figure of his father stalks
him in the thunderheads. They gather unseasonably, fields
    too wet for plowing this spring, the tobacco plants pushing
against the plastic that roofs them. A T.V. in the back room,
    after his girl friend has gone, only gathers the night
against his window, the same as when he was a child,
    afraid of it, only then sometimes his father would stand
holding him at the window in his arms, while the crickets
    subsided, and the world wheeling would pick up speed again,
turning the farm toward another day and season, but never
    toward vacancy of this same dark yet without the father.

WITHOUT DESTINATION

Tracks probed that vacuum
     like a seduction. Heat of air,
wavering cicadas, wove over rock

crust bracing the rails' double
     thrust. The depot smelled
vacant, redolent of things gone—

guano in paper, boxed parts
     of milled steel, I in short pants,
my uncle on his perpetual holiday

of summer. Teacher, he taught me too:
     the signal's green, with extended arm.
So it would come, materialize

the portended smells, oil and
     steam, air expelled, braking,
chalkish with suction. The locomotive

black as wet slate was written on
     with number and power. Cylinders
he explained in their pulse and push

hurried us down track, into horizon
     seen and unknown, color of
neuter air stunned between pines,

pure as what he couldn't explain:
     manhood of men who were busy
all seasons, with wives and sons and

no time to teach things. So we two
     sat on a train suspended in time,
he in an old and I in a young

ignorance, in the half-empty car
     for sweet gum foliage to star
past, fat in the sun, simmering

a wonder I would have to plumb on
     my own, this a trip into scent
and distance, without destination.

It led to the next town to turn
     around. I came back home
to a misery and mystery more

inarticulate than ever, guilty
        with longing. Poison ivy
leaves printed their frieze

of threes across my eyes under
        a sun in motion. The crow
flew from a sentinel pine

by the farm I would own, some-
        time. I say his name over,
like a moan. Almon, uncle and

tutor, actor in summer's scene
        of contemplation: railway
depot near my father's station,

position from which to consider,
        retire, feel and see into air, bare
eyes to water-flash and deerflies,

satisfactions in words of these.
        On a train against time, into summer,
past reason, together, we continue.

TIME AT SEVEN SPRINGS

> The literary or aesthetic act therefore always entertains some active relationship
> with the Real; yet in its own being, outside the text and at distance. It must draw
> the Real into its own texture.
>
> —Fredric Jameson

Aware of the house suspended in a riverward slippage,
    he inhabits a self invented in language, who once existed.
The boy and his grandfather approach a white, disused hotel.
    They see the Neuse, sullen in heat, icicles of Spanish moss
inverted on its surface. As Maxwell wrestles his grandfather's demijohn,
    the boy confounds their stories; remembers other conversations.
A moment lost to his consciousness rises with the voices and waters.
    In an outhouse over the river, he returns his trickle to the current.
He is one with the families who had stayed the week for treatment,
    filling the hotel. We take part in his liquid wishing, search
for the selves we were, and are; overhear as he recalls his father,
    too Methodist for the fisherman's muddy worship but aware of
Contentnea in bridge-air, an animal all tail, that might be ridden.
    Their speedboat's moment of capsize revolves in slow motion,
to bring him night: under the hull like a swallowed Jonah. He is rescued
    to consciousness, finds himself later in his grandfather's study,
wishing the awareness of Seven Springs water. In shadow, he drinks.
    Gum leaves floated red and red-green, only star-points touching
at first on the underground-seeming drainage, silt slipping like
    poured coffee or molasses, suspended in moving but always moving,
imperceptibly as the line of barn-shadow advancing in the farmyard
    as work went on and never was there time enough to finish.
A vision went out from him knowing by imagining the land he was
    now apart from. A shadow-edge detached from the eaves and
slid over cropland and orchard, elongating shade beyond the rib-
    sided farmhouses, dividing tin roofs exactly along ridgelines.
Oak leaves clung tightly to the ground as a pressure of light
    swept mule lots and the yards with tractors, laying down
figures lengthened by their passing. Heavy-armed women looped on
    the last of the tobacco. His grandfather's father, wounded
in the Civil War, disintegrated further in the graveyard across
    from the homeplace, while Toisnot Swamp a half mile away
sucked at his bones, thirsty for their decay. He feels his loss
    while it makes so complete a picture—not that the vision is untrue
but that his seeing it marks it as over. A wind blows hard over
    field rows, dusting their tops with a sugary mica, swinging

arms of cornstalks. Sweet gum balls let go their prickly holds on
      clay and flee like turned-up field mice, bumping onto pavement.
A train whistle dwindles into distance, trailing the metal vacuum
      of machines in passing, their whir and suction, as a mill-sound
busies the air and mechanical harvesters first chug their awkward
      way along ditches and crop rows. The praying-mantis combines
stoop to cotton with a reverent humming, blowing lint into bins.
      His high-school classmates face toward him, framed in albums,
fading in good-bye, those kids lean from side meat and collards,
      who went into the army, getting a little fatter, then departing
for jobs in cities, only grandmothers left, to be visited at Christmas,
      in the houses where the grandchildren's hearts still lingered.
He says farewell on paper, believing that for a region to be so
      changed it must also complete itself, that the sorrow of tobacco
will no longer haunt the soil, except from pits dug for marl
      and from burial knolls. The barns' fierce marks on horizons,
when fiery with curing, become the gesture that defined one era,
      an error necessary to discover, that his people in their history
had been driven to dress their aspirations in—those gaunt barns
      leaning hard as if to be taller against the twilight, as family
Bibles are muddied by a flood that consigns their names to the past.

Remembering William Blackburn in a Leaf

The notion of an independent truth or true world beyond the realm of
appearances is a construction or projection that grows out of the effort to
escape the flux of becoming and repress the disruptive movement of time.
—Mark Taylor

As my eye alights on the light
as it illuminates a dogwood leaf,
I ask whether sight is like what it
sees. How can the purely transparent
be akin to what obstructs it
to be known? Or how could the clear
sense of consciousness be opposed to the
objects through which it knows?
Would the moment of apprehension
divide us from our world, as by an
infinitesimal lag time of light
distancing cognition? Though the self
is enclosed in the same skin of cells
as this surface that is shining maroon,
creased by the season? Are we part
of nature and apart, awarenesses
emanated from a mud base of memory
through the red and yellow leaves on a path?
So it is movements which bring us to
these halts: October sequencings in
hickory woods alight as if Chinese
lanterns with butterfly yellow; passings
which move our perceptions like the silty
creek, fluid with undistinguished
particulars—until they freeze at
the one spot, the thought, realize the
look of the dogwood leaf, which knows
its own life, its space, this late
day in late October, after the panel
together—our remembering the great
teacher as he stood, hickorylike
in loneliness, until the last eight
years and his autumnal marriage. Today
I am halted by a dogwood leaf and
see it as itself, remembering life.

THE OTHER CREATION

A bicycle and lawnmower share the screened-in porch
    of the shrunken house. Pots of begonias, geraniums,
clutter a transition: between this couple's life as themselves—
    middle-aged, in a changing present—and this static zone
they enter, where his parents and his past live as ghosts.
    He feels his perspective foreshortened, he and his wife
silhouettes pasted in space. In the sealed air, surrounded
    by envelopes and magazines, he sees his father take a will
from a drawer. Around those pages, light deepens. Feeling
    his mortality, in the name of God Amen, his ancestor writes.
In eighteen thirty he passes on his stocks and furniture, all
    the plantation on the south side of a slough—this man
killed by lightning with his son under a tree. But mostly
    it is the slaves, the ten called by name: Feruba, Rhoda,
Sarah, Anica, Tobey, Jacob, Tabitha, Avey, Mike, and Bright.
    A son in this present is shaken by syllables from memory.
He recalls dirt streets with his father, near the railroad,
    picking up old Aunt Eliza—she of the faded headcloths,
the apron, her long-shanked footsteps shackled by pain.
    As she rides in back, he sees how another creation shaped
itself: in borrowed rectangles, shotgun cabins by the sawmill,
    wash sheds, galvanized tubs on porches, woodsmoke on
winter afternoons. He recalls the missing language, the lost
    continent of feeling. A plaque in his parents' house
holds a varnished hand of tobacco: nailed to the wood, like
    the skin of humans. The couple returns to their distant life.

Dish-shaped antennas angled toward space receive
    a microwave radiation at 2.7 degrees K
along with actors in sets: houses lacking one wall,
    through which we see these figures as ourselves—
wittier, prettier, never profoundly sad, uncertain
    only rhetorically. Do we remember memory?
Nails rust to reddish marks in soil but
    the structures which vanished may be read by
those which remain: logs squared with adzes,
    corners notched together, making expressions of windows
and doorways heavy, in those walls maybe six
    inches thick—in the unconscious, settled atmosphere
of outbuilding climbed over by trumpet vine.

AFTER *WINSLOW HOMER'S IMAGES OF BLACKS*

A Visit from the Old Mistress crystallizes into a single moment the staggering realization faced by all Southerners after the Civil War—both black and white—that things will never again be the same.

—Peter H. Wood and Karen C. Dalton,
Winslow Homer's Images of Blacks:
The Civil War and Reconstruction Years

One born where the vines coil richly, where
     honeysuckle infatuates the air, feels
memory as reflex—to be fended off, succumbed to.
     The man who is running in a Piedmont
forest has kept himself slender because those
     he was born with have bellies that stretch
their shirts. He senses a movement behind him,
     the Forest Service pickup trailing its dense
cloud in August. He steps aside to let it pass,
     covering his nose with his shirt. The dust
boils up like the steam from a locomotive—
     coming at him in a fog bank: gray, elemental,
enclosing him in a different season. A drizzle
     weighs the air, so that these cabins that don't
rise high seem taller. The doors that frame
     the figures are set in rain as in a wall.
Their lips have his name on them, and one of these,
     a matron with a chest like a rubbery valley,
brown Bit, was his mother for a time. Their head-
     cloths are blue or red, the joints of the old
ones swollen. Now they are moaning softly, it is
     the pain-song of everyday work, of hidden
selves, of roles worn habitually, to please even him,
     when he was young. His own parents stand between
the cabins, diminished in stature, as if two dolls.
     They are saying with their eyes and lips that it
was hurt and humiliation they inherited, and allowed
     him to share in—a poor fare like collards boiled
until vitamins were gone, like corn bread with flavoring
     of ashes, beans and fatback, bits of language,
in the iron pot over the open fire, in the cabin
     where the woman in her apron is stirring it,
moving the long spoon, not speaking. "Bit," he calls,
     but she has forgotten him. His memory of her

is inadvertent, resilient as beds of pine needles—
        is a smell of side meat, colored by a quilt.
The dust has gathered thickly and receded. The thin
        film left on the dogwood leaves beside him seems
a legacy which has grayed his hair and eyebrows,
        showing him at middle age for a moment like
one of the elders: those on porches who remembered.
        He continues the path before him. Through a grove,
the tire trails are that elementary farmyard
        sand, silica the rain has eroded, and beside,
brown of the loblolly needles: irreducible colors
        from his past, the pale and the brown together,
not mixing. A dove calls, bitter with pine scent.

MY COUSIN SUE'S BROAD VIEW

Rolling her neck upon the ladder back
    of chair she curved her eyes toward air
that freshened west beyond the porch, a torch
    upon her skin where sun fell plumb from
shingles hung like bangs. I couldn't gauge
    her years from eyes or from her widely open
arc of mouth, that lipped horizoned earth from west
    to east, from pine grove nested sharp and dense
to furrows and sparrows along a barbed-wire fence.
    She lolled her tongue and gasped as if her mirth
could swallow all sweet and sour of birth like biscuits
    with buttermilk. Her sister's gaze lay on us both,
lines of mouth like wire toward me but soft as her dog's
    fur for Sue, who sweltered like bread under cloth
and cursed with cleft lip in a voice that missed
    no note the choir might touch, whose body's slouch
was matched to porch and air and the sun's pouring
    and my pleasure beyond reason that July morning.
I'd come to my cousin's, his sister surprised at ease
    with the farm in her arms, that she spread
to an unembarrassed sky, plumply at home
    though her brain was said by some to be strange.
Yet for me she was large and wise as she smiled
    upon the privilege of being, that had no edge
they could push you over while you lived, no void
    to be harried into, nothing to snatch at thatches
of your hair if straw like hers, or if mine,
    like fallen needles of pine. They couldn't stop
her laugh or say she didn't belong: strong in
    her innocence, like the blank air from whence swallows
twittered later, wiggling wings, making jokes of grace.

ELEGY FOR A HUNTER

The hummingbird visits
    the cardinal flower of the garden
and you will be no more in it,

not low beneath the weave of the bees
    on watch for voles, not taking note
of my weeding, rolling in sun-ease

in your endless present. My hand
    has ended your distempered stare,
your battle gift from coon and land

still dangerous with fangs, stiff
    with stingers and poisons bright as
insects and snake-frights that ring us

in our woods house. The days will
    spin on into autumn under noons
and evenings and you no more will kill

birds and field mice, nor I feel
    your fur on my leg as you feed,
nor share your eyes' trust that no ill

would come between us in our world,
    though the rule we lived was cruel.
Now you are gone and I see you curled

in the flower bed, in my sad human
    dissent from the earth whose mercies
we remember, where graves are common.

Births and deaths were at home. Farm wives bore
     children in double beds, whose mattresses remembered
their conceptions—birth stains and death stains never
     entirely washed from pads and quilts. And though farm-
hardy, one or more of the ten or twelve would not survive—
     what with flu, scarlet fever, whooping cough, mumps,
infections when all the doctor would do was puncture
     the eardrum. With his black snap bag in his buggy,
the doctor was little more help than the preacher. Midwives
     delivered babies, neighbor women who knew how to tie
off the cord and cut it, who had talked the mother through
     the worst pain, and now handed her the red little
face just squeezed out like a pea between fingers.
     People lived and died as their destiny let them;
home remedies placated rashes with boiled peach
     leaves or a dusting of cornmeal, and fat meat
with a drop of turpentine would draw out the splinter.
     The close-fitting belly band held in the infant's navel,
and purgations with castor oil seemed a punishment
     and forgiveness of the body. Life was statistical,
for those left after the night-agony, when a wind seemed
     rushing through the house, the oil lamps flickering
at the end. All linens would be boiled and the room
     opened up to the air, the floor and the walls scrubbed.
The raw earth in a graveplot on a rise across the road
     showed a mound that would settle over years. Gradually
medicine grew helpful, with ether for setting broken bones,
     vaccinations for smallpox, diphtheria, typhoid fever.
Survivable operations began to be performed in hospitals
     in small cities: Wilson, Goldsboro, New Bern, places
of last resort, where the grief-stricken couple might take
     their screaming child in their new automobile late
at night: museumlike corridors smelling of disinfectant.
     People who had faced birth and death straight on took
parents and children to these houses of collective mourning,
     and let the white screens, the gauzes, bandage away sight
of the vagina that gaped after birth, blood trickling out of it;
     of the convulsive throes and gasps of final breaths.
But farm folk continued to surround the dying, like
     the birth giving, with a family presence, waiting in

couples and cross-generational groupings in the public lobbies,
     standing in the corridor outside the door at the end,
coming in for a last hoarse word, a hand-squeeze, a kiss
     with dry lips. And the funerals in white wooden churches
with graveside services kept on, even if the buried
     were no longer in plots in the fields, stones squared away
from the corn by fences—wrought iron softened by rust,
     no longer as hard as the blackberry bramble around it.

THE REST HOME

Everyone's urine smells the same.
That is the shame we feel,
Passing the old ones on wheels
As they foot-pull down the corridor,
Hauling what's left of life in a chair
Like a child's toy, but sturdier.

Parked by age in these halls,
They concentrate on who rolls
Best; faces wheel to watch the visitor,
Sponge-colored eyes soaking his person
For novelty, relation, recognition—
Though nothing will change this changing,

That seems endless yet suspended.
That they are so easily ended
Is the strange thing: by pneumonia,
Flu, any fever. Sitting earlier
They'd seemed perennial, fixtures
In a waiting for forever.

All smell the same, and features
That fathered or mothered one's genes
Grow to resemble, as tottering brains
Change similarly. It's a shame
We say, feeling ourselves creatures
Together in this small world of time.

THE ELECTRICIAN'S FUNERAL

The father has died. He was one who remembered when
    the steamboat huffed up to Vanceboro, with guano and fabrics.
Married at twenty, he cursed behind the mule, alone against
    the summer clouds. His daughter remembers those long walks,
taking him water, the Mason jar sweating in her hands,
    dust puffing between her bare toes. Their house near
the river had cracks in the floor, through which chickens
    might be seen in white flashes. Winters, fireplaces and
their one wood-burning stove were never enough. Linoleum
    kept part of the wind out. In summers, humidity had
the bed linens dampish, before the family retired to lie
    and sweat. During the war, he and his brother-in-law
worked for the government, wiring hangars at Elizabeth
    City. Houses the little girl saw, there and in the other
towns they moved to, seemed akin to the world she glimpsed
    in movies. She dreamed a modern life, as gradually
this father earned them stylish clothes, and a car, climbing
    poles himself, restoring the power when thunderstorms
had knocked down limbs, risking the blue fire of the current
    that sparked in streets after winds, then overseeing a crew
of linesmen unruly as convicts, some just out of jail. Later
    his marriage fell apart, his daughter helpless, an observer.
The father in retirement returned to the river and the highway
    nearby, to another wife's sad, strict house, with parlor
never used except for uncomfortable company—and to his trailer
    on the Neuse, between New Bern and Oriental, where the water-
horizon stretches to a far shore visible as a miniature
    hedgeline. There he set his net and drank, not entirely
alone in the world of T.V.'s and new cars, his buddies at
    the piers remembering also the mule plowing and bird hunting,
as they made their peace with the brown, wide water haunted
    by sailboats, taking their gill-netted croakers and bluefish.
Now with his tanned, lined features composed to a finality, he
    lies in the Vanceboro funeral home, as his surviving sisters
weep, the second wife looks solemn, and his daughter in
    a daze wanders among cousins and aunts, friends from
childhood who somehow look the same through the wrinkles and
    pudginess. Everything has changed and is the same. Roger
the double first cousin has land and prosperity, has been
    elected a county commissioner, and has had a heart attack.

Women seem hardly to have altered in forty years. Folk
    now have stylish clothes, can talk of soap opera stars.
They prosper from farming, or work in hospitals or factories,
    sell insurance and furniture. Outside their lives the Neuse
drifts widely, receiving the Contentnea below Grifton,
    dividing around islands, refreshed by Swift Creek, joining
the Trent at New Bern, surface erasing the wakes of sailboats,
    sustained by drainage from a landscape creased by ditches,
titled for inhabitancy by the boundary stones of graves.

FOR JAN, IN SEPTEMBER WEATHER

This drought is an austerity.
    Poplar leaves fall unnecessarily,
instructing in the obvious. Wild grape
    gathers its sweetness secretly.
Raccoons and possums hunt the slope
    above Seven Mile Creek
for scarcer meats. Feelings gather:
    closer to marrow, as if to discover,
to unearth the walnut, let thought
    burn lean, the wet breath evaporate.
Keen as a stretched web, delight
    breaks, this dry air focuses desire.
September weather wipes edges clean.
    Our long love cuts to the bone.

A FATHER AND SON

They have put in their canoe at Grifton.
     It may be any year but is a present, because
the man was once a son upon such water, and now is
     father. For a time, creek kinks like a snake.
Deerflies bite where they sweat. From the letting
     go of shore, they have moved in a different sequence.
Oaks and hickories become poplars and ironwoods, always
     as end to the vista—the high banks casting image
on the water, the still trees magnificent, polished,
     while underneath the current curves left, or right.
Then Contentnea empties into Neuse, like an expansion
     of vision. A house on a bluff observes with its windows.
A red clay bank where they tie and eat seems as raw as
     a memory of fever. They hunch in the grounded boat and
open sardines, too hot to speak. Later, the water widens
     and pilings from long-disused landings protrude
from August's low water. They make camp on a sandbar as
     evening comes. The father watches his son in the canoe,
anchored in the channel-middle, as light all but fails.
     An invisible line quickens the rod with meaning.
The son, excited, reels in a flashing, hauls into air
     a quiver-sided channel cat blue as horizons over
bends. As they cook this fish on the Coleman,
     lightning bugs fill the trees that ascend from each
bank: galaxies of live stars. Cicadas and bullfrogs
     voice the winding-down of August. The man is
aware that the awareness that now lights in his head
     is as brief against galaxies as these pulses of light
made by insects. Tasting the fish, he gnaws a tear-salt:
     knowing his son no better than he knew his father.
The mystery of this teenaged boy, beginning to be
     muscular, good with the paddle, is seasoned by love.
Looking at the lightning-bug stars and the close,
     real stars, he feels his mind stumble to its limit.
He feels how love remains, and hurt, salt in a cut,
     and remorse, at the memory of a life unable to extend
its spark except unconsciously, in a love-touch that
     swallowed thought and made a son. Memory of his
grandfather's bottled water hangs before him in a globe,
     like earth's whole atmosphere. Vision has circled

from water; he imagines the earth and a cell and a child
  in membranes of wetness. He drinks from the bottle
they filled at Seven Springs to begin this journey.
  The two beside the river are no longer visible
to one another. Father and son, they share the small
  tent, sleep. In the morning they are puzzled by signs
of sweeping. Beavers, clipping the willows, have pulled
  down branches toward the water, erasing footsteps.
For a little while more they print this bar with
  their shoes, before curving with the river into time.

SLENDER PINES IN SMOKY LIGHT

Bearing the pressure of light
on their high lengths, they sway
only slightly.

They point up through this
air turning blue before space,
move with the ridge as

it turns, continue their wiry
green though behind them others
whiten, bare without bark,

hollowed by woodpeckers.
Sun will be down before
I'm home. A sweet gum

makes the red sign *autumn*.
Burnt resin from where stumps
smolder a mile away

flavors the breath I suck
like quinine. Running the trail
back I stumble. The loose

rocks on the high ridge move
as if the earth had rolled
like a ball underfoot.

IMAGINARY PHOTOGRAPH

Marks of blind-shadow on
    her torso model a figure as of
marble. The stockings, removed, are
    in one hand and appear to keep
the warm body-scent, like her hair.
    Seen from below, the breasts curve
as with a texture of wind-duned sand
    and the arms are long, hair along
the shoulders chestnut-burled,
    though the face is averted, an oval:
as giantly vacant as a landscape.
    Though the skin seems to thin
under light's incision, its color
    is limestone, target of brightness,
surface ringing inwardly in layers like
    the earth's, toward a mantled core.
The fingers turn tenderly toward you,
    the nipples poignant, pointed but
blunt. The vee in hairy shading, hidden
    by cloth, half-visible, like a crevice
in rock, welcomes, as if wanderers
    on this volcanic planet-surface
could reenter rapt-dark, reclaimed.

IT MAKES A SOUND

The tree that falls in the forest
with no one there to hear it
finds me near, present/absent

the creak and pop of a limb
in wind startles
like a being, speaking

the look over a shoulder shows
so tall a thing and other
that I am lonelier

now in these sounds I utter.
Confused, I mutter *green signs,*
kings, origins.

A sense of life in both is
my surprise—like finding
an imagining.

Riverwalk with *Owl*, After the Funeral

I followed the snowflake beat
    of a wool owl's flight
falling wing by wing on
    the coming night—as if circling

a seeming surface of air, its
    aqua reflection. He perched
in pine branches cleft like
    rafters of a vanished house,

then ruffled up his overcoat,
    a ghost, charring that site
where attic and chimney had gone
    and briars grew over the stones.

My uncle upstairs in our house
    his summers as vagrant teacher
once whooed his Halloween travels
    no more alone than *owl*.

I whispered *Almon, Almon*
    as a charm against his breath's
mistake. Sound alone rounded
    the clearing, mirroring light.

Consoled by the sky's slick
    lake, I felt his loneliness
and hurt cease to haunt.
    Words were our common lot.

I climbed down the ridge to
    the stream, seeing across and
into my own life, where a yellow
    window meant my wife.

There, an echo-halloo shadowed
    the air blue, like water.
I was not far enough from home
    to hear any lonelier color.

A Mark in Sunlight

In my residence on earth
    I feel the February crust
(flat and curved, from stone

and alive) as it heaves itself
    newly along its course
among the stars. Buds race

to risk a cold that spring
    thinks only intrusion, though
the carbon dark of space

remains infinitely frozen.
    In the yellow of our
close star, jonquils follow

this arc of re-beginning,
    as if this breath-warmth
on faces were the first to

burst the calyx and chrysalis,
    as if this moment I sit
in the shade of an oak trunk,

delighting in light, were
    the first I noticed shadow
move its mark as I watched.

Unsettled, I shift my chair,
    aware of the sundial edge
as it measures this warmth

of a lifetime. The tree's shaft
    cast on the yard, fixed
amid the whirl, brushes the grass

as it spins with the planet:
    straight and slight as a soul,
like the pole of my awareness.

I breathe in tune with an air
    that holds Earth's warm and cold
and yellow, cups each moment

with a flower. This fear is part
    of the praise, seeing our sphere
curve sight among the stars.

The Village After Sunset

The Town of Stantonsburg grew up at the intersection of the Waynesboro-Tarboro road and Contentnea Creek. Where these two arteries of transportation met, the Stanton family built a landing. From this landing naval stores, cotton and other produce was shipped down stream to New Bern. Fertilizer and other supplies from down stream were landed here.

—A History of Stantonsburg, ca. 1780–1980

He remembers the village after sunset as in
    a space of gold leaf. Once nativities with
angels lay as flat against a sky thinned
    by time as this Protestant congregation,
rinsed by their hardship, waiting on new shore
    for revelation in a star. Their honest faces
had overseen the storefronts and steeple,
    houses determined in the squares and peaks
by need to keep heat and shed rain. Now
    light seeping back into space raised the town
into a flat elevation, like the set for a Western.
    That absolute contemplation, that tabula rasa
of light, stunned his mind. Simplicities
    occupied vision like fruit in a still life.
Revelation came not out of all-radiant
    space but from caves in the body. Animals
in their stables witnessed births of animals.
    Passageways showed where road or river
had framed a perspective. Only along these
    did change unfold, in a skin like a snake's:
an oily hieroglyphic writing a slither of
    becoming into scenes as if embroidery—
the house, the pickets, an oak with the leaves
    in cloud-shapes, as sun arced over in its
varying constancy. The well rope went
    down into a circular gaze, but this other
look brought the steamboat, in a simple
    apparition, out of bends of pure reflection.
The sun so flooded the senses in its synchronic
    origin, his eye had not imagined far sources.
The fierce blade of harvest and carpentry
    cut the serpent as it twined into innermost
recesses. Desire had unfolded without wisdom,
    following cascades in their musical cadences

when the spring flood had let Contentnea
        spread near the bridge, like an expansion
of vision. Then the packet came up as far
        as Stanton, bringing laces and fabrics.
An organ had rested perilously on the deck
        during the whole trip upriver from New Bern.
Christmas that year heard voices more nearly
        those of angels: children in the nativity
wearing aureoles of tinsel, as gold-leaf sunset
        framed the town in its permanent being.

THE WAYS

It was a man with beard who knew
    and cared and then it was a *them*:
the ones whose rules and ways around
    extended with the town, in attitudes
we lived among—a crowd yet one—
    older and like forever in their seeing.
Then space they used to fill with gaze
    grew wider and thinner, a center as
where the pebble hit the pond expanding
    into circumferences of stars,
with nothing to fill it now, no name
    or scripture except sometimes the rain:
its steadiness suddenly on the window
    as I feel its extent, its falling over
the river and the houses on the far shore
    and its hushedness in the dwellings
of all the hearers of its spinning
    of these lines of a mist in which we
breathe our belief in rain and leaves.

What You Don't See Is There

The hundred-year oak curves aside
      in its suppliant gesture, though others
that shadowed its growing have rotted
      to stump holes. So history twists in
my psyche. Amputated limbs and thwarted
      wills walk fields of the mind; rubble
of cotton gins and tin barns follows
      footsteps through woodland: these farmed
rows and erosions with trees reclaiming
      them buried in memory. A wounded land
warns sons and ignores them, praises
      daughters it adores, whores, makes kitchen
drudges of, loving itself slightly, sadly.
      Virginia's burnt horizons with chemical
factories fume marshes of self-defeat.
      The fatback lies lean among snapbeans;
pokeweed, no longer eaten, edges pastures,
      with barbed wire ingrown in trees like pain.
This poem presses its vision into dirt as if
      a seeing phallus, thrusting toward solace,
though the blindness of the past chokes with
      its refuse: the slapped negress, raised dress,
the tipped vagina, the murdered owner, this
      stripped land washboarded by rain, crows
seen on fields through windows, the mules'
      stiff walk in mornings, smoke rising,
those mourning the corn bread and chopped wood,
      the working for nothing, for another year,
the meal coarse and the dress of feed sacks,
      the ten-year-old fondled, confused, wedded
to family wishes, dishes, and washtubs. This wish
      is for clearer air, for feeling not colored by
heroes as lightning-struck trees: bark flayed
      away like skin, smoldering resin, clouding
love's vision, the horizon-flavor bitter.

THE RIDGE ON THE EDGE OF DAY

Behind my house the ridge
    of Seven Mile Creek raises
its edge against the farther sky
    in twilight. As Canada geese
vee over I feel its trees fledge
    this soil over stone as if plumes
or veins, extending its life's purpose
    into the draining air. I feel the world
wheel my house with its dreams into darkness.
    Tonight on this shelf above the creek it is
my privilege to walk and think this thin
    edge where the dark ground is bounded by
faint light and trees without leaves feather
    their illegible purpose in a scrawl whose
total I see is whole if beyond my knowledge.
    Tonight I am content to be a creature lent
this riding with the movement of the planet since
    across the noise of water is my wife, whose
kiss will ease the mystery as we face night together.

TIME IN AMERICA

Houses have a quality of already.
      Their sheen tin lends a speculation
to wedges that will rust like thatch.
      Horizon hovers shapes all seen before—
though simpler here, under new air. Stones
      like blunt gnomes in groves by the road
name graves. These Margeries and Mildreds
      dress trees under vapor with memory's
idolatry. Long wed and buried, honored
      in what they said, they suffered beddings,
sexual wettings, a story all told before.
      A field's far shore holds a house like
rubbed bone—whose windows gauntly
      encounter this country: the pasture
empty; leaf surfaces like pond patinas,
      under clumped late-April pecan sprays.
A baby never filled the interior, the heart's
      bright mirror-me, mirror-me, when
marry was only waiting on, sating needs
      or serving: no mother able to season dishes
on table with her self's bitter sprinkle.
      The mustard greens looked blackly back,
the crows arose, the smoke curled wispier than
      did their daughters' hair. Quilts came
square by square, until the rectangle
      of stone. These houses bloomed alone,
their old world soul shaped in wood
      and tin, in strict chapels, revivals.
So time in America passes, progresses.
      It was and is again, pure of
color in weathered board and tin, in
      roofs to hold the sky's truth among
pastures of clover. Stories of sin shone
      clearer here, transparent as water,
the black snake's quick mark only
      a fright, a darkened lightning.
Their rising up and lying down, opening
      of womb and dying, are written
in plowed land and pasture, in framed
      stones by the road that prove their

loves and gods in simple phrases—
    in dates, finally, the earlier and later.
This is why the trees must hover
    over. Faces show in marble surfaces
like daughters' reflections in water.
    The grace of their dresses is vapor.

LIGHT'S PRAISE

Light which is my being in the world
    while others aren't, how you strike
the leaf, which frost has thinned like skin
    (translucent to your probing, veined),
my thought still tender with the wound of
    what is not and what is yet. Light,
in my years left in the sun, let me rise
    within excitement, knowing, like a body
from a dive, breaking surface continually
    into your pinpoint minutiae of stars,
your early coming to dew and birdsong.
    Harp me, responsive to your praise, permit
my lips through your returns to speak an
    awareness that extends to farthest stars,
from tissue of leaf lit green within.
    Light, existent from the start, not to be
extinguished by my or anyone's exit, circle
    on yourself, oh self-subsistent seeing, await
new leaf to illuminate. Infuse my doubt,
    glow in the sphere of your nature.